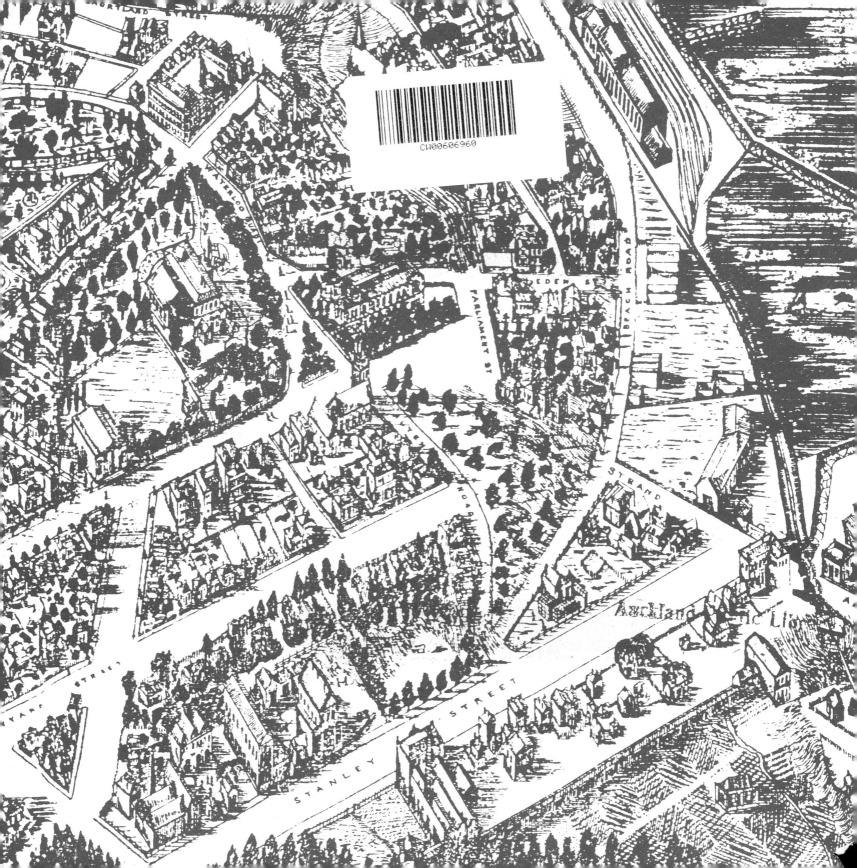

To Cecil Lewis

from your colleagues
in appreciation of your contributions
to the School of Medicine
during your Deanship
(1966-1974)

25th Anniversary

1968-1993

Michael Fowler's
UNIVERSITY *of* AUCKLAND

Michael Fowler's
UNIVERSITY of
AUCKLAND

MALLINSON RENDEL

For
Amanda, Brooke, Pamela,
Rex, Olivia, Kitty Hamilton
and January's child.

First published in 1993 by
Mallinson Rendel Publishers Ltd
P.O. Box 9409, Wellington

ISBN 0-908606-87-7

Typeset by Wright & Carman Ltd, Trentham.
Printed in Hong Kong.

Contents

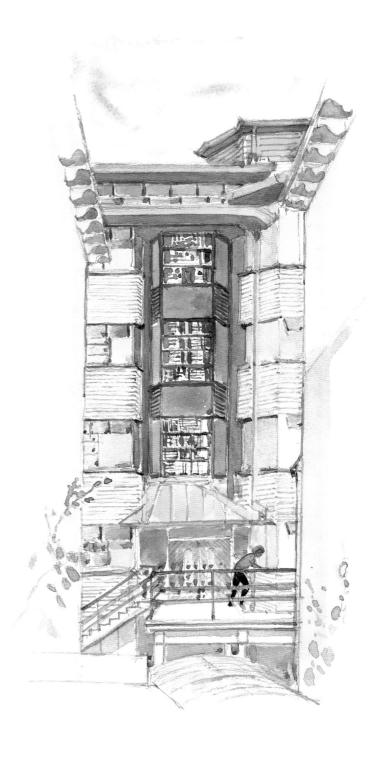

Acknowledgements

I am very grateful to Sir Keith Sinclair for allowing me to refer so often to his excellent *History of the University of Auckland*, published in 1983, the University's centenary year. I hope that this much shorter essay will encourage readers to seek further knowledge of the campus' history from Sir Keith's volume. I am also grateful to the New Zealand Historic Places Trust, A. H. and A. W. Reed, the L. D. Nathan Group of Companies, Auckland University Press and Grantham House for allowing me to quote from and refer to their publications, which are listed in the bibliography.

My particular thanks are given to my Auckland architectural colleagues who have provided me with encouragement and information during this project. I include amongst them Ivan Mercep of JASMAX, (till 1990 known as JASMaD, an acronym of the founders' names, Jelicich, Austin, Smith, Mercep and Davies), Denys Oldham and Ian Reynolds of KRTA, and Professor Allan Wild of the School of Architecture. The latter two, enthusiastic and knowledgeable, have been towers of strength to me, and have read and advised me on the manuscript. Indeed, Ian Reynolds drew the cross-section at the foot of this page to illustrate the campus topography. The mistakes that remain, however, are all mine. But then, the pleasure in sketching this book has all been mine — I appreciated meeting young undergraduates and staff members while I sat around the campus sketching, for they seemed interested in what I was doing, and appeared to be enjoying their involvement at the University and on their campus.

Princess Street

Preface

Auckland friends asked me to join them in setting up an Alumni Association for their university. It was my university as well, so I did.

During the last few months, while we were getting organised, I found time to walk around the campus: the old Arts Building, Old Government House, the new School of Architecture built on the site of the army huts which formed my School, and many of the areas on the Symonds Street saddle which have changed so much in forty years.

If I were asked which are the four most beautiful parts of the University campus today, I would answer Symonds Street, Alfred Street, Old Government House lawn and Albert Park. And so it was when I was an undergraduate, except of course that the lawn was then denied us, but we coveted it and I went as far as planning a football stadium to replace Government House. May I be forgiven.

Of my other three preferences, the University encompasses both Symonds and Alfred Streets, and Albert Park will inevitably be surrounded by the University in due time.

I became so entranced with the quality of light, the colour and character of the city streets within the now extended campus, and with the delightful openness of Albert Park that I decided to sketch these major elements of the University.

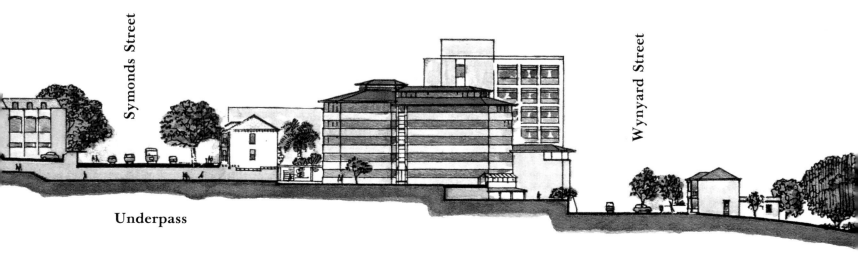

That led me to look again at Lippincott's 1920s Arts Building, at KRTA's Thomas Building and its secret courtyard, and the School of Architecture atrium. It became an obsession. I sketched the campus buildings on either side of the Symonds Street ridge, and the buildings in the general environs out to the edge of the campus, most of which are so much a part of the history and ambience of this lovely site.

The University of Auckland was certainly frustrated in its birth and adolescence, far more so than its colleague universities of Otago and Canterbury, even Wellington. Whereas the southern cities were passionately supportive of the establishment of their universities, the pragmatic citizenry of Auckland could hardly have cared less. The birth and site acquisitions of the University led to a series of unforgettable brawls of the sort that wrack Auckland regularly.

When Bury was designing great stone buildings for Otago University, and Mountford was designing the Canterbury quadrangles, Auckland University College did not even exist. Finally, in 1883, it began by occupying the unused timber Parliament Building.

The Auckland University campus has become a city campus. Straddling the saddle between the Queen Street valley and Grafton Gully, it is intimate with and dominant in the central city, being far more a city university than its New Zealand peers. Canterbury fled the city to the suburbs of Ilam, a frightful mistake, and Otago and Victoria Universities, while on their original sites, are only loosely related, even visually, to the central city area.

I found the Auckland campus fascinating. Some of the buildings are excellent, and some are not. Is it not always so? But I thought its brief history, including its tenuous start, the story of some of the characters who moved it along into its eventual massive expansion, and the buildings and spaces which have marked that progress, might make a worthwhile series of sketches in words, and in pen and wash.

I've enjoyed doing just that, and have also enjoyed the people who have helped me. I hope the result may encourage others to see the delights of this unique city campus.

1. The First Forty Years

THROUGH his advocacy, one Aucklander became the focus for the creation of an Auckland University—George Maurice O'Rorke. Graduating in 1852 with BA (Hons.) in Classics at Trinity College, Dublin, he migrated to Victoria, working first as a digger on the goldfields, and later on sheep stations. In 1854 he came to Auckland with a college friend, Henry Taylor, who subsequently became Secretary and Inspector of Schools for Auckland. O'Rorke farmed at Papakura and Onehunga. He successfully stood as a parliamentary candidate for Onehunga in 1865 and, with two three-year breaks, remained the member until 1902.

His political prominence provided a platform for his promotion of an Auckland University. Some, however, would say that his ardour outstripped his political sagacity. He advocated as early as 1872 that the proposed New Zealand University should be established in Auckland as a teaching and examining body, that the Old Government House and grounds in Auckland be dedicated to the university, that all monies voted by Parliament for universities should be divided equally between the university in Dunedin and that proposed for Auckland, and that Albert Barracks and some adjoining land be made a university endowment.

These radical proposals, while eminently sensible, were like a red rag to a bull to the Cantabrians, well advanced as they were in establishing their own university, and their continued opposition to O'Rorke and his ambitions was a definite hindrance to his university plans. Not that he was without opposition in Auckland. Following the lead of one of Auckland's prominent merchants, J. C. Firth, who stated that 'over-education is one of the curses of this age', the *New Zealand Herald* trumpeted in 1881 that it thought 'a good grammar school more important than a pigmy university'.

In reply, the *Auckland Star* said these views 'were a monstrous libel on the community' and lamented the fact that the absence of a university did not seem to trouble Aucklanders.

What really did trouble Aucklanders in the 1880s and for the next eighty years, was the possibility of Old Government House and its grounds going to the University. The city smarted for decades at the loss of its capital status to Wellington and, with it, the domicile of the Governor-General. Many Aucklanders hoped to see the Capital reinstated on the shores of Waitemata Harbour, and the Governor-General reinstated in Government House in Auckland. Long after that option was lost, William Mason's Government House remained a symbol of that forlorn hope.

Had O'Rorke not linked his proposed Auckland University to Old Government House, it is probable his ambitions might have been realised earlier. In 1878, Sir George Grey's Government appointed O'Rorke chairman of the Royal Commission on Education. The other members, five professors from Dunedin and Christchurch and four members of Parliament, possessed a wealth of experience gained in European universities. O'Rorke's opinions were heeded, and amongst the commission's principal recommendations were that university colleges should be established in Auckland and Wellington.

In 1881, Bills were drafted to give effect to most of the commission's recommendations, and these were enacted. But by this time, the colony's economy was faltering, and Parliament chose to vote only £1500 for the University College, sufficient possibly to obtain the proposed four professors, but the inadequate sum meant that the University College would exist for years in rented premises, and questionable ones at that.

The Minister of Education, Thomas Dick, instructed the Agent-General in London, Francis Dillon Bell, to engage the services of at first two professors and subsequently a further two, at £700 a year each. With the welcome assistance of distinguished scholars, such as Benjamin Jowett, Master of Balliol, Bell performed admirably, and the new University College obtained a most impressive quartet: Frederick D. Brown for chemistry, Algernon Phillips Withiel Thomas the biologist (after whom is named the Thomas Building), Thomas George Tucker the classicist, and George F. Walker for mathematics. Walker was tragically drowned off Shelly Beach soon after his arrival, and was replaced by William Steadman Aldis.

The paucity of the University College accommodation was mirrored in the residential accommodation which the four professors had to find for themselves. It must have compared badly with the 'venerable pile' of Otago University's stone building, designed by Maxwell Bury and built in 1878-79, let alone the splendid brick professorial houses built in 1879 for Otago's first four professors, Shand, Sale, Black and Scott.

In 1898, the indefatigable Sydney and Beatrice Webb visited New Zealand, principally to examine the trade union movement, the arbitration court establishment, and local government. However, their interest in education caused them to spend some time at Auckland University College, then in its fifteenth year.

Beatrice diaried thus:

> The University College is housed in the quaint ramshackle wooden buildings that once served the infant colony for Parliament House and Supreme Court. [These bordered Eden Crescent and looked out on to the first St. Pauls Church.] Its income is £4,000 government grant and £800 fees. It has 83 matriculated students, and about 120 attendants at courses of lectures. Nearly all the students are teachers actual or prospective, and have little time or inclination for intellectual work. The half a dozen professors—entirely English university men—seem well paid—the chemistry man gets £800—but lack stimulus. The Auckland business and professional world seem to supply practically no students—not even the unemployed daughters. The University has clearly failed to make itself popular in any sense—attracting neither endowments nor students other than teachers. No joint action with Christchurch or Dunedin—the other colleges of the New Zealand University—in fact, mutual jealousy. No Political Economy taught—Classics, Mathematics, Science, Literature, French, German—but no Philosophy or any other subject of intellectual stimulus beyond a secondary school course. Many of the lectures given in the evening to suit teachers engaged during the day: and these by themselves enable a man to take degree after examination.
>
> Our general impression of education as shown in Auckland: seedy in appliances, imitative of old English models in method, honourable and gentlemanly in its spirit but quite without originality, independence, or modern ideas.

Eventually, Prime Minister Seddon was convinced by both O'Rorke and another Auckland University College Council member, F. E. Baume, recently elected to Parliament, that the Auckland University College needed further buildings. In 1905 £5000 was allocated.

The Auckland University College Council, consistent, yet naive, advised that the Metropolitan Ground (a somewhat grandiose name for the cow paddock/sometimes football ground) which adjoined Old Government House, was the preferred, indeed only, site for the University. While George Hogben, the Inspector-General of Schools, agreed with the University College Council, and strangely so did the *New Zealand Herald*, the Auckland Scenery Preservation Society did not. The society, analogous to the 'Greenies' of today, declared that this green open space should continue to be available to the citizens of Auckland. This argument was fallacious since the land, like Old Government House land, was Crown land and not, as of right, open to public access.

Seddon's viewpoint was seldom directed by conservationists, and his enthusiasm for the site was greatly diminished when the Governor, Lord Plunket, objected. He then replied to the Council's application for the 'Met' site with a telegram that read 'Impossible'.

Eventually, the Crown provided four thousand pounds for the University College Council to buy the Choral Hall in 1907. The Council now owned two parcels of land: the site of the old Parliament Building, and the site of the Choral Hall.

In 1909 Prime Minister Joseph Ward advised the Governor, Lord Plunket, that the Government required the land on which Old Government House stood for a University College and other public buildings. This time Lord Plunket acquiesced, allowing that the house was an old wooden building, and the grounds were neglected. Little did he, or Ward, foresee the opposition which would be mounted to this proposal.

The opposition was marshalled in the first instance by T. W. Leys, editor of the *Auckland Star*, who promoted the sharing of the 'Met' ground between the Grammar School and the University College, and wanted hands-off Government House. Public opinion was roused both by the *Auckland Star* and the *New Zealand Herald*, in a way that newspapers today would find impossible, such chicanery being the preserve of radio talk-back hosts.

In September 1910, the *Herald* smugly wrote: 'The settlement of the university site question has naturally taken the form repeatedly suggested by the *Herald*'. That settlement was to allow university buildings on the 'Met' grounds, which

The old Choral Hall, purchased by the University in 1908 and extended in 1918.

12

were judged more than sufficient for such purposes. ' It leaves the city and province in possession of a very cherished institution (Old Government House), in threatening which the Government made a grave error.'

But that was not the end of it. Within a year, the *Herald* was trumpeting that 'there is probably in the minds of those so eager to secure the Metropolitan Grounds for a college, the hope and intention of finally securing the whole of Government House grounds . . . The Mount Eden site is an admirable one in every respect—large, imposing, central and commanding . . .' The newspaper continued in a similarly droll vein to include the need to immediately construct an alternative gaol 'in a more secluded part of the Dominion . . . The really magnificent tract of land on which the Boys Grammar School has been assigned as a new home, to which other beneficent instructions may arise, will then be altogether creditable to the metropolis and will commendably adorn the central position it occupies.'

The public was eventually sufficiently aroused by the *Herald*, and by a self-promoted group named the Citizens League, to gather a petition of 20,000 signatures against 'the taking of any Government House grounds'. Nevertheless, the University College Council voted for the 'Met' site, and so did the City Council, six votes to five. Then in 1912, the Liberal Government resigned to be followed by William Massey's Reform Government. Massey's view was that it would have been better if the University had selected another site. The wheel had turned the full circle.

By 1914 the University still owned only the Choral Hall site and the old Parliament Building site in Eden Crescent, and the latter was required for roading purposes by the City Council.

O'Rorke, in his 85th year, was now very much in decline, and often absent from University College Council meetings. He had long ceased to be an effective contributor but was still held in some awe. Hindsight would have it that he should have withdrawn from public life years before. He died in 1916. His successor, T. W. Leys, editor of the *Star*, was the University College Council Chairman from 1916-20, and lent enormous impetus to the progress of the University site issue. He held the Council on course, rejecting another government offer of forty acres in Mt Eden, leased the now deserted Grammar School in Symonds Street on the site of the present School of Architecture, and for an expenditure of twenty five thousand pounds made up of seventeen thousand pounds compensation from the Auckland City Council for the old Parliament Buildings, and eight thousand pounds savings, made substantial additions and alterations to the Choral Hall. It became the first permanent home for the University, though it housed only about one third of the students. It was opened in 1919, and later that year the government agreed to provide the 'Met' site. Perhaps surprisingly, there was now little opposition.

Keith Sinclair suggests that people were simply fed up with the dispute, and that the prestige of the University College in the community was by now higher.

In any event, the government now offered £100,000 to the University College so it could begin planning for buildings to house its other departments on the 'Met' site. All these events were greatly to the credit of Leys, and 1919 is the year that set the seal on the University's occupation of the Princes Street — Symond Street site.

Yet it could never be assumed that the 1919 decisions were inviolate. Forty years later, the site row exploded again, and the same rancour, buffoonery, chicanery and irrelevances cluttered the media, the University College Council, Parliament and the Planning Tribunal until the site was finally re-affirmed.

The Northern Club, 1967 designed by James Wigley

14

2. *The Environs*

WHILE the University College was consolidating its small and tenuous land holdings on the Princes Street — Symonds Street ridge, other uses for nearby areas of land were becoming established in the public mind.

The most obvious, of course, was Old Government House. A large area of land had been set aside by the Government for a residence, garden and horse paddocks for Governor Hobson in 1840, when it was decided to transfer the Capital from the Bay of Islands to the Waitemata Harbour. Hobson's charming timber home, prefabricated in London and not dissimilar to the Waitangi Treaty House as we know it today, was burnt down in 1848.

Five years later, the Executive Council promoted a competition among architects for the design of a new Government House in Auckland. Reader Wood, the Deputy Surveyor General, was judged the winner, with two of his staff, Charles Heaphy and James Baber second. However, the Executive very soon had doubts concerning Wood's competency, and instructed the second place winners to prepare detailed estimates of their plans.

William Mason wrote immediately to *The New Zealander* criticising both designs for inadequacies of construction. All parties then publicly criticised their competitors' entries, with Heaphy and Baber stating that Mason had forgotten to take ground floor chimneys through the first floor and roof, and had arranged a twenty-four inch (61 cm) brick wall, unsupported over his dining room. All this was heady stuff, but Mason did prevail, and in late 1854 was appointed architect for Government House.

In the biography *William Mason, the First New Zealand Architect*, John Stacpoole suggests that the Wellington members of the Assembly moved to hold the 1855 session 'in a more central position in the colony'. This was nearly successful, and considerably frightened the Aucklanders who moved with some alacrity to expedite the construction of a new Government House on the premise 'that a satisfactory residence would at least endear Auckland to the Governor, and where he lived the Capital would be'.

Old Government House.

Mason benefited from the urgency. He wrote to the acting-Governor, Colonel Wynyard, proposing that it might be better to consider building the Residence of scoria rather than timber — 'maintenance, insurance and fire risk would all be greater with a wooden building. Stone would be available from Mt Eden.' However, timber was insisted upon. This accorded with Governor Hobson's original intentions that this Government House, being of a temporary character, might afterwards be converted into public offices 'whenever a permanent mansion should be thought advisable'. Hobson's view, which he expressed to Lord John

Newman Hall entrance on
Waterloo Quadrant,
originally Bella Vista, the
home of David Nathan.

Club bought the building in 1869, Edward Ramsey, the architect of the Supreme Court building, was retained for the large alterations and additions. Later, in 1884, Reader Wood is understood to have designed the new dining-room and the fifteen bedrooms above, which look out over the city, and are hard against Bankside Street. There is a telling, if somewhat thin, oil painting of Sir John Logan Campbell in the Northern Club dining-room, arrayed in a long red cassock — quite startling really, until I realised it was the nineteenth century mayoral robe, which taken up, looked a bit moth-eaten on my much shorter friend Robbie, (Sir Dove-Myer Robinson) some eighty years later.

The University subsequently established itself and expanded into the ridge lands between Princes and Symonds Streets, where many of the successful Jewish merchants had earlier built their homes. The original Auckland Nathan, David, arrived in Auckland from Kororareka in 1840, and with the help of his brother-in-law, Moses Joseph, established an Auckland retail store close by Commercial Bay which is now reclaimed land forming Quay Street and Customs Street. Their first store was close by the present corner of Shortland and High Streets. David Nathan was immensely successful as a merchant and well regarded by the entire Auckland community. He died in 1886 at Bella Vista, the home which he had built in Waterloo Quadrant, and which is now Newman Hall.

David's second son, Alfred, lived in Wickford, the large plastered brickwork home at 24 Princes Street. When he died in 1931, aged 81, the home was sold and became a nursing home until bought by the University. It is now the Registry. David's first son was Laurence David Nathan, who established with his brother and family the firm L. D. Nathan and Company which for so long was at the forefront of wholesale business in New Zealand.

Princes Street, Waterloo Quadrant, Symonds Street, Alfred and O'Rorke Streets were highly prized and valued residential properties, and many were occupied by successful Jewish families such as the Nathans, Myers, Benjamins, Keesings, Moses', and Davis'.

Albert Park is a glorious tree-filled space overlooking the heart of Auckland. Visually, and actually, it is an integral part of the University campus, often used by students for relaxing on the lawns, and certainly as a garden through which to walk on the way to or from the city.

The band rotunda, built in 1901, is a charming piece of Victoriana, set in its tree-enclosed sloping glade. There are other delightful Victorian elements such as the 1881 fountain, the Helen Boyd memorial marble statue of Love breaking the Sword of Hate (unfortunately broken for her and stolen in 1985), Queen Victoria herself, and one of her noblest of servants, Sir George Grey, who lost his head again in 1985, after which it was retrieved and fastened permanently into place.

In my time, the Auckland Central Police Station was sited in O'Rorke Street. That agreeable street disappeared in the 1960s, becoming incorporated into the campus, and the strange new Police Headquarters building was erected on the opposite hill across the Queen Street valley. The vast Science Buildings, also designed by the Ministry of Works architectural division, now occupy all that area between the previous O'Rorke Street, and the parallel Wellesley Street East.

For many years, three of the four campus corners were marked by houses of worship—St Andrews on the north-east, the Synagogue on the north-west and St Pauls on the south-west. The latter great Rangitoto blue-stone church, designed

The eastern sanctuary of St Paul's Church looming over the Elam School of Fine Arts grounds.

26

St Paul's Church in Symonds Street, adjacent to the Wellesley Street off-ramp from the motorway.

27

by the architect W. H. Skinner, replaced the earlier St Pauls designed by William Mason in 1841.

The site of St Pauls slopes steeply to the east, and the sanctuary, which was not built in permanent materials until 1936, is necessarily a very high structure, looming over the Fine Arts School environs. When I was sketching the two-floored brick building opposite St Pauls, which contains a coffee house called the Wynyard Café, well-frequented by students and staff of the University, I was sitting on a small lawn beside the church. Every time a bus or heavy truck passed on Symonds Street, the ground shook, and so did the church. Though there is little evidence of structural damage, there can be no doubt that St Pauls is disadvantaged by the vast excavation on its northern flank which contains the Wellesley Street on-ramp.

The south-west corner of the campus, when I was an undergraduate, was also marked in secular fashion by the Wynyard Arms, a tavern much frequented by students of the School of Architecture which was opposite. In the late 1950s, the hotel's name was regrettably changed to The Kiwi, and even more regrettably, it was demolished in 1989. The site remains empty.

Newman College, Melbourne University, designed in 1916 by Walter Burley Griffin and Roy Lippincott prior to Lippincott's arrival in New Zealand.

28

3. Roy Lippincott

ROY LIPPINCOTT won the competition for the new Arts block for the University College. When the Government agreed to give the 'Met' site to the University College in 1919, and offered £100,000 for an Arts building, the University College Council was at last able to act.

Of the forty-four designs submitted in the 1921 competition, that of Lippincott and his colleague Edward F. Billson was selected. Lippincott was a junior partner of Walter Burley Griffin, the designer of Canberra. Griffin's sister was Lippincott's wife. They had all relocated in Melbourne from the United States when Griffin won the Canberra competition, and were all involved in the 'Prairie School' in Chicago, and therefore directly influenced by Frank Lloyd Wright. This is evidenced in Melbourne University's Newman College which they designed, and of course is also apparent in the Auckland University Arts Building.

This building is of reinforced concrete, sheathed in Mt Somers stone from Canterbury. The formwork, construction, concrete pouring and subsequent stone-sheathing of the finer elements of the clock tower tested the ability of the contractors, Fletcher Construction, and their subcontractors. A. C. Marshall, later senior lecturer in construction at the School of Architecture (1938-67), is credited with detailing the tower formwork.

Though the siting of the building, and the prominence of the clock tower, virtually axial with Victoria Street, added immeasurably to the Auckland townscape then, as it still does now, the design engendered 'a roar of protest'. It was criticised for not fulfilling the brief, for torturing spaces to conform to the exterior symmetry, and for inadequate services and lack of provision for future expansion.

The Education Department architect, Mair, was critical of the tower, which he thought un-British. He also said that the ends of the wings would be improved with turrets, and that he preferred rooms off only one side of the long corridors, as in primary schools. Even the Minister of Education, C. J. Parr, suggested the building would be quite satisfactory without the tower, which when erected drew the droll comment from the poet A. R. D. Fairburn that it would frighten

Lippincott's Tower from Princes Street.

30

The stairhall of the old Arts Building, under the Tower.

*The old Arts
Building cloisters
by Lippincott.*

33

old ladies in the park. Happily, the welter of criticism when Lippincott's design was selected, and during construction, deterred neither the University College Council nor its chairman Sir George Fowlds, and their steadfastness was well rewarded, for the building very soon became highly regarded by both Aucklanders and students. It was opened in 1926.

Lippincott's incorporation of New Zealand native flora in the arches and bosses led to the critics referring to his Maori Gothic structure, but time has ended such remarks, and it is well worth taking a careful look at the delightful forms he incorporated in the stonework details.

The Custodian's Cottage (1928-30) by Lippincott.

The old Biology/Zoology
Building designed in 1938
by Lippincott.

35

Lippincott's extension to the Old Choral Hall.

36

27 Princes Street,
substantially altered by
Lippincott in the 1930s.

37

The original brief, and therefore the Lippincott drawings, included no facilities for the students such as cafeteria, student association rooms, lounges and the like. But during the contract, funds were raised, including a generous £10,000 from the Auckland Savings Bank, and the student wing was added, being the two-floored addition to the east, linked by cloisters to the main building. While these cloisters are reasonably practical, they are not as successful as those in Newman College at Melbourne University.

What is highly successful is the centrepiece of the tower, not only as a symbol of the University and a major element in the Auckland townscape, but also as the circulation centre of the Arts Building. The stairhall at the lower level of the tower is superbly fashioned outside the supporting columns of the tower, and the mosaic tiled floors and carved stonework are entirely complementary to the overall design.

To the east of the Arts Building is a two-floored cottage, designed for the university custodian by Lippincott. Now overshadowed by the adjoining Thomas Building, which caused a portion of the east end of the cottage to be demolished, and jostled by the two Commerce buildings, the cottage nevertheless stands pleasantly and solidly after sixty years, redolent of a simple Voysey design which may have influenced Lippincott.

The third Lippincott building was opened in 1939 by Peter Fraser, at that time a very successful Minister of Education. It is the 'old' Biology Building, fronting on to Symonds Street, and directly behind the Arts Building. Originally three floors of reinforced concrete, a fourth floor of a most unfortunate steel-clad, vaguely Mansard-roofed form was added later to the building's detriment. The original colour was a creamy pink, with red trim to window frames and sashes, but in the summer of 1992 the building was repainted, which is laudable, except that the walls are now a lolly pink. The building is essentially very simple with two flights of stairs at the quarter points, fair face concrete walls slightly buttressed at the corners, and arched heads and deep reveals to windows. The patterned concrete at the entrance porches again incorporates symbolic abstractions of local flora. On the stairways, delightful cast bronze snails support the round wreathed handrail.

Roy Lippincott also designed an extension wing to the Old Choral Hall, and substantially altered Number 27, one of the five houses opposite the University in Princes Street. Other buildings designed by him include the new building of Smith & Caughey which faces Elliot Street in Auckland, St Peters School at Cambridge, and the original Massey College Buildings (1929-30).

In 1939 he and his wife left New Zealand for a visit to his homeland, the United States, but the outbreak of war caused him to settle there after a brief return to close his Auckland office.

4. The Thirty Years War

AFTER the completion and occupation of the new Arts Building, designed by Lippincott in 1921 and opened in 1926, the majority of the students, their professors and lecturers were more reasonably housed.

The Sciences continued in the extended Choral Hall complex, to which a further wing was added in the neo-classical style, designed by Lippincott. This was far from his normal field of expertise, but he had studied the form of the other additions, and had clearly enjoyed his research for his addition is in great harmony with the other parts.

Even the Conservatorium of Music (now the School of Music) which had been the orphan of the University College since its inception in 1888, enjoyed reasonable accommodation for the next twenty-three years in the new College Hall, where all music lectures and recitals could be held.

Despite its improved accommodation, the Auckland University College suffered along with the rest of New Zealand during the ensuing depression from 1928-1935. Keith Sinclair, however, believes this was a time of awakening.

The students, who by 1930 numbered about 1200 on site (there were also 140 extramural students), became less conservative politically, and more conscious of their rights. The staff, leavened by new appointments, began to advocate their own rights to freedom of expression and in so doing ran headlong into the conservatism of the University College Council. During this time, Auckland lost the brilliant young lecturer J. C. Beaglehole, whose one year contract was not renewed following his criticism of the restrictions on expressions of opinion imposed by the Council's president, G. W. Fowlds.

Fowlds had followed Leys in the presidency and, as had Sir Maurice O'Rorke and the best known of his successors, W. H. Cocker, he gave an immense amount of his time and undoubted talent to the running of the University. These extraordinary men all seemed to become totally absorbed by the challenge of their positions. While in theory the Council's responsibility lay in determining policy, it also devoted endless time to the management and administration of the

The remnant of the Albert
Barracks Wall, built
between 1846 and 1852, to
the north of the University
Library. The completed wall
originally enclosed twenty-three
acres of land.

40

University. Subsequently this became awkward in the extreme when the Council finally appointed a chief executive, first called the Principal, and later Vice-Chancellor.

In the 1930s the students objected to the Council over Beaglehole's loss, over Professor Worley's somewhat vague lectures, and publicly and noisily advocated academic freedom. The attitude of the Professorial Board and the staff also hardened against Fowlds, O'Shea and the conservative members of the Council. But there were still professors and staff who were right-wing adherents, one of these being Professor Ronald Algie, later Minister of Education in the Holland Government. There was division in the ranks among the students, the staff, the Professorial Board and even the Council members. In a way, New Zealand was growing up, and suffering growing pains which were exacerbated in the atmosphere of the University, where truth, the search for it, and its pronouncements meant different things to different people within the campus.

Sir George Fowlds stayed on until the fiftieth anniversary celebrations of the University in 1933, small though they were in those penurious times, and then he retired. The Registrar, Rock O'Shea, stayed on for another four years, but in truth his power had waned. His reactionary attitude was increasingly questioned by students and staff alike, and his withdrawal was inevitable.

Fowlds was followed by two short-term presidents until 1938 when Hollis Cocker assumed the Chair, which he occupied for the following twenty-three years. Like Fowlds, Leys and O'Rorke, he bound himself to the University College with an intense loyalty, and gave enormous time to its management and advancement.

Students and graduates of the last thirty years can have little comprehension of how appallingly the University College was housed in its earlier years. Even with the new Arts Building, the extended Choral Hall complex and the Biology Block, certain disciplines remained greatly disadvantaged. The present lawn, to the north of the Albert Barracks wall near the Library, was for decades covered with the most outrageous collection of temporary buildings. A large part of this area, now known as the Barracks Wall Green, was occupied by the 'Tin Shed', a corrugated iron-sided building erected for the School of Engineering as a ten year temporary measure in 1908.

When I was an undergraduate in 1950, the engineers had forsaken the Tin Shed in disgust two years before, and moved to the disused airfield and buildings at Ardmore. Before Professor T. D. J. Leech moved the Engineering School from the Auckland campus, a distinguished visitor, Dr F. Dunsheath, Member of Senate, University of London, described the building as being 'more in the level of a bombed London College', and pronounced it 'a disgrace to the city and to the University'.

It is worth noting that as the School of Engineering moved out of these disgraceful premises, the School of Music moved in, occupying these 1908 temporary buildings from 1950 to 1969.

The outbreak of the Second World War in 1939 brought about a decline in student numbers from 1400 to 980 in 1942. By 1945 the numbers rose to nearly 2300, and in 1948 had increased to 3400. There was a great number of returned servicemen, some in their mid or even late twenties, and in many cases these students were highly motivated, attempting to make up for lost time.

In 1948 the University College Council made a pivotal decision, namely to appoint its first Principal. The method of selection and appointment was chaotic, and made even more so since the Council and the Professorial Board were once again at loggerheads. Nevertheless, an appointment was made, that of a classics don, Kenneth Maidment, Sub-Warden of Merton College, Oxford.

Maidment began as Principal in 1950, and his worth was quickly appreciated by Council members and professors, though his greatest problem was with the president. Apart from his puritanical manner, Hollis Cocker had for years been acting both as Vice-Chancellor and Registrar, as well as Chancellor. He expected to decide or at least to participate in decisions on every policy matter, whereas in Maidment's view a chancellor was merely a ceremonial figurehead.

The truth lay somewhere between these polarities, probably a bit closer to Maidment's standpoint. A good vice-chancellor would obviously prepare policy options for his council, and guide them in their selection. A good chancellor would keep well clear of administration, yet in the long tradition of involved presidents at the four university colleges, and in Auckland's case of O'Rorke, Leys, Fowlds and now Cocker, the latter found the new regime as difficult as did Maidment. Clearly this did not help matters during the revival of the site row.

In a way, that matter had been determined when the Council had accepted the Government's offer of funds for a new biology building in 1936-37. The President, T. U. Wells, and the majority of the Council at that time were in favour of the Princes Street site. Wells argued that so much had been spent on the site that it was too late to change.

Having made that decision, the Council then decided again to ask for Old Government House. The Government refused until the University College had the support of the Auckland City Council and 'some support in the city'. The City Council donated nearly half a hectare of land in Alfred Street to the University College, but since the Government made no further move, the University College Council decided to purchase, with £14,000 of its own funds, 48 hectares of farmland at Tamaki. This was a strange move, for already the University College was consolidating on the Princes Street site. But, in 1944, the Council turned aside from that, deciding that the University College should relocate to the Tamaki site. By this date Cocker was president and, with his allies, was the dominant

The University Registry at
24 Princes Street was
known as Wickford while it
was the home of Alfred
Nathan, the second son of
David Nathan. After 1931,
the house became a nursing
home, until purchased by the
University in 1938.

force in the Council. Thus was the gauntlet thrown down, and the second great site row erupted, not to be resolved for another sixteen years.

It should be noted that the Tamaki site was good land, well-drained, overlooking the Tamaki estuary and part of the Hauraki Gulf. But it was remote from the central city, at least eight kilometres away, and although there were plans for a rapid-rail link, no such transport mode eventuated, and never will. The distance made the Tamaki proposal unacceptable to the large number of part-time students (64 percent) who worked in the city. It was also unacceptable to staff and students who believed the role models most suitable for universities in New Zealand were city universities in the United States and the United Kingdom, rather than an ivory tower campus in a rural setting.

The debate split the Council, the staff and the student body, and engendered considerable rancour between Auckland citizens and their City Council.

The Labour Government approved the move to Tamaki in 1949 with conditions such as no further building on the Princes Street site, and no more than one major building constructed at a time at Tamaki. This was a Clayton approval.

Even the National Government, which won office in late 1949, approved the Tamaki move despite Ronald Algie, previous Professor of Law at Auckland, being the Minister of Education and having always been a 'Princes Street site man'. In 1954 the same Government approved the first Tamaki building, the School of Engineering, which had been incarcerated in the wilderness at Ardmore for five years.

But by then, the University College Council had begun to lose enthusiasm for Tamaki. There was no sign of the rapid-rail link and, without that, the site was virtually inaccessible to students and the public. At the same time, enormous pressure was mounting in these post-war years for accommodation for lecturers, staff rooms and services.

In 1952, I was the President of Arch. Soc., the architectural students' society, and the clear opinion of that group was a preference to stay and expand on the Princes Street site. We produced drawings (one of mine being a football stadium on the site of Government House which causes me some slight anguish today) which *Craccum* published, and we wrote articles expounding our argument.

The Students Association arranged a debate that year, the pro-Princes Street school headed by the School of Architecture, the opposition led by the engineering students. One could hardly blame them, isolated in the dreariness of Ardmore, in tin army huts. Mind you, the entire School of Architecture was similarly housed in army huts but in Symonds Street.

The engineering students, numbering about fifty, came in from Ardmore to Princes Street in a bus. Through the simple ploy of extending the meeting by interminable speeches (engineers as a rule are boring, but that evening they

44

excelled themselves), they were able to win the debate. All other students were forced to leave to catch their last bus or tram home, but the engineers had their own bus and, immediately they had a majority, forced the vote, boarded their bus, and retired for another seventeen years to Ardmore. They next appeared in their new Symonds Street School of Engineering in 1969.

A somewhat unquantified offer was made by Sir James Fletcher in 1955 to reclaim Hobson Bay, and build a series of exhibition halls for a proposed 1966 World Exhibition which the University College could subsequently sub-divide with partitions. That the Council was a confused body by this time is evidenced by its ready acceptance of this harebrained scheme. No definitive estimates of reclamation or construction costs were available. The Hobson Bay scheme eventually sank in late 1956, as surely as the buildings would have on the proposed reclamation. But for a while the Council, the staff, the students and the newspapers supported it, then finally went off the idea. Meanwhile, nearly another two years were wasted.

In August of 1956, Algie approached Council with the news that his Government was now prepared to give Old Government House to the University College, which should accept the Princes Street site as a permanent home. In addition, the Government would make £750,000 available for a new physics and chemistry building. By a majority, the Council voted to accept the offer. However, those known to have voted against were Dove-Myer Robinson, then an Auckland City Council representative on the University College Council, Cocker, Maidment and Henry Cooper, the headmaster of Auckland Grammar.

What was to be a climactic row broke across Auckland, student against student, staff member against staff member, citizen against citizen, the *Auckland Star* against the *New Zealand Herald*.

The then University architects, Massey Beatson Rix-Trott & Carter, prepared a preliminary overall plan and the University College Council approved it early in 1957. While some Council members such as R. G. McElroy, were forcefully vocal in support of the Princes Street site, others were equally public in their opposition to it. Douglas Robb was one, and even Cocker was criticised by the Government for being less than enthusiastic in his support of his Council's resolution.

The Auckland City Council was against the Princes Street site, as was SPACE, a lobby formed by Dove-Myer Robinson called the Society for the Promotion of Academic and Cultural Education. Douglas Robb was a member, as were Professors V. J. Chapman, botanist, and Kenneth Cumberland, geographer. It was strange that these latter two were so publicly against the Princes Street site, since the University College Council and the Professorial Board had voted in favour and continued throughout to support it.

The University Club, 23-25 Princes Street, sketched from Albert Park.

The National Government was voted out in December 1957, Walter Nash became Prime Minister, and P. O. Skoglund Minister of Education. Even when the report of the Ministry of Works on Hobson Bay was published three months later, estimating the reclamation costs at three times more than the Sir James Fletcher estimate, the University College Council inexplicably voted ten to six to ask for this to proceed as the favoured campus site. This asinine decision sent Phil Skoglund scurrying to Auckland, where he approved the purchase of several old houses in the Princes Street area. Later, even Walter Nash accompanied his Education Minister to Auckland, where they both inspected Princes Street and Hobson Bay. Surprisingly, Nash reached a decision, and in late August Skoglund stated that the Government would not proceed with Hobson Bay, and that the old Government House site would be added to the campus (again!).

In October, the University College Council voted again, this time eleven to six to stay in Princes Street. Maidment, by this time frustrated beyond belief with the impasse, voted with the majority, but Cocker, Cooper and Robb, along with a Presbyterian minister, Owen Baragwanath, a chemist, and the Auckland City Council representative voted against. The dispute, which in effect began in 1872, dragged on with gathering acrimony until 1960. In that year the Auckland City Council lodged an appeal before the Town Planning Appeal Board against the designation of the Princes Street site for the University. Such a designation had been required to be incorporated into the City Council's District Scheme by the Minister of Works, Hugh Watt.

Keith Sinclair describes how Roy McElroy wrote to Skoglund at that time: 'If I may say so, I would urge at all costs that the University Council be not entrusted with the task of making the submission on behalf of Princes Street. In the first place they will not know how to do it, and in the second place they will not have the will to do it.' This was a damning indictment indeed, and evidently well heeded for the Government mounted a powerful submission by the Ministry of Works, represented by the Solicitor-General, H. R. C. Wild, Q.C., assisted by excellent witnesses such as Professor Kennedy and the young architect and planner Ian Reynolds. Professor Kennedy was highly critical of the City Council for making no reasonable study of the growth pattern within the central city. Keith Sinclair quotes him as saying at the hearing: 'Within the proposed ring road could be found at present every imaginable use, ranging from new ten-storey offices to car dumps, half built and abandoned structures and some of the most dilapidated obsolescent buildings—residential, commercial and industrial—to be found anywhere in New Zealand.'

The campus plan presented by the University College before the Appeal Board was an amalgam of a scheme prepared by Robert Matthew in 1959 and the University's architects Massey Beatson Rix-Trott & Carter. Matthew was the Professor of Architecture at Edinburgh, architect for New Zealand House and many universities, and had been invited by the University College Council to visit and advise. The University architects incorporated many of Matthew's ideas in a revision of their own earlier works, and this formed the submitted proposals to the Appeal Board.

The somewhat specious arguments by the Auckland City Council and their witnesses and counsel were very quickly identified by Wild, and subsequently by the Appeal Board. The City Council's appeal was disallowed, and the University College could lay claim to its site, and develop it.

The traffic control to the campus on Symonds Street, the power base of gatekeeper Ralph Wood.

48

5. *The Building Boom*

THE certainty of the university site at last allowed progress to be made on a long overdue building programme. Definitive site plans and schedules had already been prepared, but were immediately over-turned when Skoglund suggested to Cocker that the School of Fine Arts could be erected on vacant Crown land on the periphery of the Princes Street site, close by the present Wellesley Street off-ramp. The land is low-lying, beautifully treed, and accessible either from Whitaker Place or by pathways from Symonds Street behind St. Paul's.

The Elam School of Fine Arts had come under the jurisdiction of the University College Council in 1959, up to which time it had been an independent art school. The director was A. J. C. Fisher, and he somewhat surprised the University College by preferring his friend A. R. D. Fairburn, the poet, over other applicants in 1950 for the position of lecturer in the history and theory of Fine Arts. As Sinclair writes, 'Fairburn was a remarkable character, whose qualifications in art history were, however, obscure'. Fairburn himself thought his chances of appointment were extremely slim, and in a letter to a friend wrote: 'If I were to go abroad, drink steadily for twelve months, buy a black homburg and a big pile of coloured postcards of the masters, and come back again, I should no doubt be considered a gift from Heaven to the art school'.

The architects for the building were Massey Beatson, and the subsequent library additions were by the same firm, now practising under the title Curtis, Penman Read and Williams.

I enjoy the site, particularly the north lawn with the giant canopy of the oak tree creating an enormous outdoor studio. To the south of the 1963 building, through a low-lying grove of trees, are the 'Mansions'; one an old two-floored, brick building with timber verandahs on the north front. It is used by Fine Arts students for their personal studios. Twenty years ago, when I was preparing a thesis for my Masters degree, I would often visit my tutor Imi Porsolt who had rooms in this brick building. He had organised an opening between two adjoining rooms through a double brick wall, and his eyes shone with excitement when

The School of Fine Arts Library addition.

50

The brick 'mansion', now part of the School of Fine Arts.

he advised me it was exactly one metre wide, and two metres high. These generous metric dimensions appealed far more to his European background than did our meagre imperial measurements. When I sketched this building from below, I rushed the exercise as I was ferociously savaged by hundreds of mosquitoes, and both my hands were swollen for days.

The other building on this site is of timber. Both buildings were boarding houses and hostels for many years before the Crown acquired them for the University in 1971. The timber building was, reputedly, in its earlier years, the home of Gottfried Lindauer (1839-1926), an artist who devoted a great deal of his talent to portraying the Maori.

Apart from the massive building programmes of the 1960s, the University College came of age in other ways. In January 1962 it became independent. The New Zealand University was disbanded, and each of its colleges gained autonomy. The new Act also changed the structure of the University Councils, requiring a greater representation of professors and lecturers, and insisting that all academic appointments and dismissals be referred to the Professorial Board, which now became known as the Senate.

A further amendment of particular interest to Auckland University was the limiting of the term of a president to two consecutive three year terms, and a person could not be eligible again for that office until after a three year absence. Thus there could never again be a continuous O'Rorke, Fowlds or Cocker.

Hollis Cocker retired in 1961, and Douglas Robb, a surgeon, and the deputy-president, succeeded him as the Chancellor in 1962. Vice-Chancellor Maidment described him as 'a most awful nuisance—he took too much upon himself, he assumed the Chancellor had a function, which he did not'. However, never one to be denied, Robb threw his energy into the establishment of a medical school in Auckland, and since it was widely considered to be a reasonable idea (except by the Otago Medical School), the proposal eventually succeeded, due not so much to Robb, but to the brilliant analysis and submissions of Wilton Henley, Superintendent-in-Chief of the Auckland Hospital Board.

Once the concept was approved, a gradual acquisition of land began opposite the Auckland Hospital in Park Road. Building started in 1968 and was to continue for 10 years. The architects of the Auckland Medical School were Stephenson & Turner, originally an Australian partnership which developed a reputation for hospital designs in the 1930s and 1940s. They were invited to New Zealand to assist with the planning of hospital extensions in Otago in the 1950s, and their practice expanded into Auckland and Wellington thereafter.

The Medical School as now completed will last for a hundred years. While sketching it, I was delighted to talk with some medical students who appeared very cheerful, despite having just left the dolorous series of heavy grey buildings which make up the Medical School. Perhaps that is a bit unfair—Ian Reynolds

quite properly argues for its muscular articulation and skilfully detailed surface textures. It is, he says, a child of its time.

Although the Old Government House grounds were not formally deeded to the University until 1969, two new university buildings spread on to these grounds prior to that year. The first was the McLaurin Chapel, close to Symonds Street, in amongst some of the lovely trees of Old Government House grounds. Fortunately, one seldom sees the building in relation to Old Government House, for it is very much of the 1960s, being a grey concrete octagon with heavy, white-painted timber joinery, and a flat-roofed, schoolroom-type addition. It pays no

The Medical School through the Domain Gates designed by Gummer and Ford and sculptor R.O. Gross.

53

The Pink Cottage,
Auckland Hospital,
with the Medical
School beyond.

55

The Thomas Building from the bus stop in Symonds Street.

57

regard whatsoever to its renowned neighbour Old Government House. The chapel was designed by Gummer Ford & Partners, and was opened on 23 March 1969.

Sir William Goodfellow donated the building to the University in memory of his son, Richard McLaurin Goodfellow, who was killed in action over Norway, and also in memory of Richard's uncle, Richard Cockburn McLaurin, a brilliant Auckland graduate who became president of the Massachusetts Institute of Technology. The University accepted the gift, though a condition was that it would never be a place for Catholic instruction or worship. Twenty-five years later, this prejudice begins to rankle.

The second building to extend on to Old Government House grounds is the Thomas Building, named for the foundation professor, Sir Algernon Phillips Withiel Thomas. He was twenty-six when selected in 1882 to become the first Professor of Natural Sciences at Auckland, and had already solved the problem of the liver fluke while working for the Royal Agricultural Society in England. In later years, while at Auckland, he became internationally known for hybridising the daffodil, and in his retirement he made a fortune from forestry shares.

The massive University Science Buildings on the north of Wellesley Street East.

The University Library opened in 1969.

The Thomas Building is sited against Symonds Street, and is chiefly positioned on the 'Met' site, but its northern section extends on to the site of the old stable yards and kitchen gardens of Old Government House, carefully avoiding any elements of the mature landscape. Designed by KRTA, the building is a reinforced concrete frame of four floors, clad externally with massive, U-shaped, precast concrete spandrels of a sandy pink colour. The building is thus highly textured, a slightly heavy-handed but witty exercise in precast concrete. It is built around a central courtyard, which is its most pleasant element, for it is well proportioned, producing a micro-climate which greatly favours the abundance of vast tropical plants which thrive in it. The courtyard is provided with screens, stairs and water features, which along with the planting are a delight. I regard this courtyard as one of the University's best kept secrets. First occupied in 1968,

A staircase in the Student Union complex by Warren & Mahoney.

the Thomas Building is used in conjunction with its southern neighbour, the Biology Block designed by Lippincott.

The Science building was a three-stage development, the first stage being that part near the intersection of Wellesley Street and Symonds Street. Designed by the architectural division of the Ministry of Works, this large series of structures is very much of the 1960s. Exposed scoria aggregate panels contrast with the fair face concrete, as do the basement and plinth walls of natural stone. The buildings are very heavily modelled. Time has not enhanced a lot of the fair face concrete which is stained, not so much by the atmosphere but by poor detailings of throatings, drips and other weathering details. The interior spaces, particularly the main circulation areas, are fairly ho-hum, but nevertheless, the Science

*Grafton Hall, opened in
1969.*

The School of Engineering by KRTA, opened in 1969.

62

buildings have a style and panache which, while a bit dated, are strong, and confident.

This could not be said for the Library building which, up till 1992, also housed the Law School on upper floors. Designed by Massey Beatson Rix-Trott and Carter, the massive building completely overpowers the delightful Alfred Street which it fronts, and employs a strange array of clip-on sun screens, and flimsy, vertical balcony struts which unsuccessfully attempt to disguise a plan and structure of consummate ordinariness. A splendid opportunity was missed but the building, completed and occupied in 1969, most certainly fulfilled a long denied requirement of the University to have a large, centrally located library. It currently houses over 1,300,000 books, and is a most efficient and valued centre of the campus.

The fourth major campus building constructed concurrently with the other three, during the late 1960s, was the Student Union complex. The students abhorred the idea of a tall structure, and wanted a series of low buildings around courtyards, and this is indeed what Miles Warren and Maurice Mahoney designed. Warren & Mahoney designed student centres at Canterbury and Massey Universities as well, all crisp articulate buildings of fair face concrete and white-painted blockwork. The Auckland example fails in parts like the curate's egg. The small structure modules become monotonously repetitive, allowing too little flexibility of spaces. It was conceived with a student roll of 5,000. Now, in 1992, the roll is over 20,000. It is clear that the buildings and the spaces they encompass are grossly over-filled, and major extensions are inevitable and necessary.

The first major building across Symonds Street from the main campus was the School of Engineering. The engineering students and staff moved into this long awaited building in 1969. These premises on the corner of Grafton Road and Symonds Street are excellent, especially after sixty-three years in tin sheds and disused hangars. Designed by KRTA, the School is centred around a concrete tower of eight floors with lecture theatres and laboratories disposed below, using the falling ground to the east to great advantage. Restrained, yet intelligent design has provided the campus with a good example of a reinforced concrete and blockwork building in which the changing demands of the faculty are met, and the anonymity of the forms allow the drama of the great Symonds Street trees to act out their seasons and colours without competition.

During the 1960s then, five major buildings were constructed on the Princes Street campus: the Thomas Building, the Library, the first stages of the Science buildings, the Student Union complex, and the Engineering School. Approval for a building for the Human Sciences was sought and granted by the Government, and approval in principle was granted for design work to begin on a School of Architecture and Town Planning. Both of these proceeded in the 1970s, one more successfully than the other.

In 1969, a new hall of residence, International House, was opened. The

The lower courtyard tennis court at International House (1969) by JASMaD Architects.

64

buildings are pleasantly located on the steep hillside overlooking Grafton Gully to the east, and are intelligently arranged about an upper courtyard and a lower tennis court. Designed by JASMaD Architects, International House accommodates 164 residents, and is sited in Whitaker Place off Symonds Street.

Another hall of residence for university students, also accommodating 164 residents, but not owned or administered by the University, is Grafton Hall, and it too was opened in 1969. The concept was the vision of Dr David Williams, Principal of Trinity College, the Methodist Theological College in Grafton, the building now occupied by 'Professor' Whitecliffe's Art School. Williams saw a better potential use for the three Trinity College tennis courts a little downhill from the college and, with other Protestant clerics, and the University, set about forming

The School of Political Science occupies these three Victorian houses at 12, 14 and 16 Symonds Street.

65

the P.M.C. (Presbyterian, Methodist, Congregational) Foundation. The idea of an ecumenical hall of residence proved attractive and, designed by Haughey & Fox, the building was opened debt free in 1969.

The simple form of the ten floored hostel building stands out dominantly on its high site. A centre corridor gives access to the rooms which face east and west, looking out to panoramic views of Auckland, and one assumes that the happier students are those who do not suffer from agrophobia since the sill height of all windows is the floor. The building is ageing well, after nearly a quarter of a century.

Parallel with the building boom, the University, with the co-operation of the Crown, continued to acquire existing houses in Symonds Street, Grafton Road, Alfred Street and Wynyard Street. These houses were pressed into immediate use for sections of university departments or faculties, and originally this resource was considered temporary. However, many of the staff found the houses made delightful offices and tutorial rooms, and came to prefer them to space in the new buildings.

The Political Studies Department was one such group which temporarily occupied numbers 12, 14, and 16. Number 12 was built about 1885 as a solicitor's home, and in the 1920s, in common with many Symonds Street homes, became a rooming house. It was constructed of pumice concrete. Number 14 was acquired by the University in 1967, and was built about 1900. Number 16, built about 1890, was previously known as the Arras Private Hotel and became university property in 1964.

When I was sketching these houses in Symonds Street, two political scientists I knew, Andrew Sharp and Graham Bush, came out and invited me in for coffee. They told me how the staff, learning of the future available space in the vast Human Sciences Building under construction in 1977, immediately advocated the retention of the three Symonds Street houses they were occupying, and they were successful. The retro-fitted buildings are delightful, though some serious cracking is appearing in the external walls of Number 14, no doubt due to the increasing volume of heavy traffic on Symonds Street.

The formal acquisition of Old Government House by the University occurred in 1969, eighty-eight years after the Government in 1881 first proposed to transfer the site for future university use. The building immediately provided space for a senior common room, reception rooms, and flats for visiting scholars. The architectural firm of KRTA designed the refurbishment of the building, and in recent times have restored the central pediment from the altered triangular form to its original segmented shape. They have also had the hood removed which disguised William Mason's three central round-headed windows. An external colour scheme is most successful, but the tonal grey paint of much of the interior woodwork leaves many observers a little bewildered.

67

The addition of the Old Government House grounds to the campus immeasurably increased the greenery and open space of the University. A great deal of the campus was well planted already, the botanists having been happily involved in the directing of this, and in 1968 the University retained a highly regarded Danish horticulturist, John Eiberg, to maintain and develop the grounds. A number of specimen trees in Old Government House grounds were planted over a hundred years ago, some by Sir George Grey, and these add scale and a sense of history as well as enclosure to the great lawn fronting Old Government House.

Viewed from city office towers or the upper rooms of city hotels, the Princes Street site appears one great forest, pierced here and there by the taller university buildings and of course Lippincott's clock tower. This image is assisted by the proximity of Albert Park, and the avenues of poplar trees in Princes Street and plane trees in Symonds Street. There are no parts of the campus which can rival the Yard at Yale, with its spaced 150 year old trees providing a summer canopy to the building-encircled lawns. But the Old Government House lawn is a great assembly space, well used formally at graduation time when the Alumni Association provide an enormous and elegant marquee, and informally during the academic year by both staff and students for strolling and for picnics.

The lawns, gardens and trees of the campus and Albert Park, along with the trees in the campus streets—Princes, Symonds, Alfred, Grafton, and Wynyard, even Whitaker Place—and the adjoining Domain, provide an ambience very particular to this country, and the city of Auckland. This, in my view, celebrates a coming of age and maturity, and marks the regard in which this centre of learning and research is held by the community it serves.

6. *Challenges of the Seventies*

T WO MEN had a strong influence on the University in the seventies. One was Allan Wild, appointed Professor of Architecture in 1969. A graduate of Auckland University College School of Architecture, he had worked in Auckland and Wellington in the private and public sectors. The other was Colin Maiden, appointed Vice-Chancellor from the beginning of 1971, on the retirement of Kenneth Maidment. Aged 37, he was a former Rhodes Scholar from Auckland University where he had graduated in engineering. At the time of his application he was in charge of several research departments at the General Motors Technical Centre in Michigan.

Wild's architectural input to the development of the Auckland University Campus was immense and greatly valued. One wonders what input if any had been made by the School of Architecture during the 1950s and 1960s, apart from advocacy for the retention of the Princes Street site, as opposed to the Tamaki site. Prior to Wild's appointment, the three professors of architecture, Light, Woodward and Toy, had sat on the appropriate committees. They became known as the three wise men, like Trappist monks maintaining a vow of silence.

From 1969 Allan Wild, as well as being Dean, provided the Senate and the University Council with the professional advice expected of a senior and reputable practitioner, and the University from then on retained the best architectural practices in Auckland to design and supervise the necessary buildings in accordance with professionally prepared briefs. His contribution to the orderly, strategic planning and expansion of the site began with his 1971 campus development plan which made a comprehensive attack on the Symonds Street barrier by means of cut and cover grade separation.

However, many projects had already been committed in the 1960s, such as the third stage of the massive Science Block on the corner of Princes Street and Wellesley Street East. This powerful final stage of the Ministry of Works architectural division's design was completed and opened in 1972. The whole of the grouped Science Buildings make a fairly daunting statement from the 1960s.

The vastly oversized, precast concrete elements, the almost Cyclopean scoria stonework at ground level and the immense, scoria-faced spandrels seem to diminute both student and observer. I found it more comfortable to sketch this forte of the sixties from five hundred metres' distance, namely the top floor of the new Centra Hotel in Elliot Street.

In 1969, approval had been given by the Government for the planning of a new School of Architecture to replace the series of metal clad army huts which had housed the School for nearly two decades, and it is clear that Wild had a controlling hand in the successful complex which eventuated, along with the architects KRTA. That series of buildings was not completed until 1979.

Another major building approved to proceed to planning in 1969 was the Human Sciences Block. The site is the east side of Symonds Street opposite Lippincott's old Biology Block. The architects were Massey Beatson & Partners. Like the School of Architecture, its ultimate realisation was delayed until 1979. It is difficult to appreciate the very large scale of this complex from Symonds Street, for it is screened to some extent by kerbside trees, by many Victorian residences retained along the frontage, and partially by the more recent JASMaD designed Commerce C Building on the corner of Symonds Street and Grafton Road which wraps around the southern end of the building. However, from the east, that is from Parnell and the Domain, and particularly from Wynyard Street which it fronts, the gargantuan scale of this building is very apparent.

One hopes that the interior of the building may be better, but it is worse. There are low ceilings, ungainly shaped foyers and endless corridors, but the views from the building's upper floors are dramatic. This building was the last of the campus dinosaurs, an enormous 1950s concept, sketched in the 1960s, and completed in the late 1970s.

Dr Maiden looked upon the challenges facing the University with fresh eyes. He noted immediately the lingering animosity between town and gown, which had been exacerbated by the great site row. He also knew that student facilities were virtually non-existent.

This concern was speedily addressed in the 1970s. At first, there was a minor flurry centring around the reclamation of Hobson Bay (again!), this time for university playing fields, but this aberration was halted by the Student Union who, voting on the issue, preferred Tamaki for their playing fields. Eventually then, the University benefited from its wartime purchase of the Tamaki land for a campus. The University sold some of the Tamaki land, and with the proceeds, expanded by reserve funds, developed what is now called University Park. An area of 16 hectares, it is well landscaped with football and cricket grounds, grass tennis courts and excellent pavilions and clubrooms. Apart from the rugby clubhouse, KRTA designed all the landscaping and buildings. The delightfully landscaped grounds off Merton Road are separated from the University's Tamaki

The Conference Centre above the School of Architecture Library with the studios beyond.

campus by Morrin Road, which at the separation point is depressed in a cutting; thus a level bridge at grade can eventually link the Tamaki campus with University Park.

The University allowed the New Zealand Commonwealth Games Association to build temporary structures on the empty campus site to form the Commonwealth Games Village for the Games in early 1990. Most of those timber buildings have been relocated elsewhere, but sufficient remain, and have been adapted to form

The School of Architecture from the Wellesley Street off-ramp.

The Human Science
Building from under
No. 12 Symonds Street.

73

the nucleus of temporary accommodation for the four hundred or so undergraduates located on the Tamaki campus. An architectural brief is being prepared for a staged development of this campus, which is anticipated to accommodate two thousand undergraduates in the year 2000. This brief is being prepared by KRTA, JASMAX and Boffa Miskell.

Not far from the Tamaki campus, which enjoys high ground overlooking the Tamaki estuary, is the Auckland University Rowing Club. The building is no doubt adequate, and is a vertical board and batten-clad, three-gabled structure of about forty years, with a certain charm, and a happy proximity (but not direct access) to the estuary and the nearby Panmure Boat Club Pavilion. It was designed in 1952-53 by Ivan Mercep, his first commission on graduating.

At the same time as the University Park was being developed, the University set about the construction of a large on-site recreation centre. The site allocated was 17 Symonds Street, immediately east of the Student Union Buildings, and the architects chosen for this commission were JASMaD (now JASMAX). This was their first major involvement on the campus though they had earlier designed International House, the student residential hall on Whitaker Place.

Their selection has been justified on three counts. Firstly, the Recreation Centre, with a floor area of 4650 square metres (most of which demands a clear floor to ceiling height of 8 metres), is a vast volume, which in less sensitive hands could have grossly overwhelmed both the Student Union buildings, the surrounding courtyards, and the adjoining Symonds Street.

The way JASMaD handled this commission, by virtually excavating it into the ground so that only one floor level projects above the campus courtyard level, is like the way Posokin handled the Palace of the Congresses in the Kremlin. Posokin deliberately restricted the height by excavating deep into the ground, so that the palace is no higher than the nearby Arsenal building. The Kremlin survived the containment of the Palace of Congresses, and the campus survives the containment of the Recreation Centre.

Secondly, the architectural merits of the Recreation Centre were very quickly recognised by the architects' peers. JASMaD were awarded the NZIA Gold Medal for its design in 1979, one year after it was opened on 11 May 1978 by that best of Ministers of Internal Affairs, the late Allan Highet (who died today, 27 April 1992, as I write this).

Thirdly, the building has proved immensely popular amongst the students, both as a sporting and fitness centre, and also as a gathering place. When I was sketching it, I noted its environs were particularly favoured by the Maori and Polynesian students as a place to forgather. But the proof of the success of the building has been a continuing and successful partnership between the University and JASMAX.

Colin Maiden's further thrust in the recreation field was to see that the theatre

The University Recreation Centre by JASMaD Architects with Symonds Street and the School of Engineering beyond.

76

complex, always planned to be part of the Student Union area, was progressed. The architects Warren & Mahoney were retained, and fittingly so, since they had already prepared sketch plans for this art centre in conjunction with the Student Union buildings in the 1960s. The resultant building, which is on the corner of Princes and Alfred Streets, is very much in sympathy with the Student Union, being of an exposed, reinforced, concrete frame, and white-painted blockwork. Named to honour the University's first Principal and Vice-Chancellor, the Kenneth Maidment Arts Centre contains the Kenneth Maidment Theatre which seats 440, and the Little Theatre which seats a hundred, both of which proved very successful venues for university and other groups of performers.

The same architects designed and supervised the second stage of the Student Union building which was built by Calder Construction Company in 1973. It is interesting to compare the Student Union accommodation after the completion of Stage I in 1968, with the previous space allocated to the Union from 1926 to 1968 in the east wing of the old Arts Building. Of course the numbers were less in my time—in the early 1950s, about half. Nevertheless, we enjoyed the building and its cloisters. In a way, it was an oasis of permanence in a desert of the most appalling tin sheds and shanties which filled every ground area between the Arts Building and Symonds Street.

Subsequently, a great deal of the rubbish was cleared out, some of it replaced by the two buildings known as Commerce A and Commerce B, designed by Beatson Rix-Trott Carter & Co. in 1958. In defence of the architects, for the two buildings are abysmal, these two-floored, steel-framed structures, clad with flat asbestos sheet, and battened, now thirty-five years old, were virtually temporary structures. One hopes that they have now served their purpose, and that before long both buildings will be blown-up, pushed over, or otherwise removed, thus creating a reasonable open space in the heart of the campus which will allow a sunny, lawned area for relaxation.

It would also enable one to better appreciate the three surrounding buildings by Roy Lippincott which began the campus: the Arts Building, the custodian's cottage, and the old Biology Building. The sloping lawns towards Princes Street and Old Government House could provide a stepped amphitheatre for viewing staged, evening productions from the east wing of the Arts Building, and seating for the increasing number of students during lunch-times. The subtle floodlighting of the Lippincott buildings, the Barracks Wall, the appropriate parts of the old Choral Hall and the Thomas Building, and of course the trees, could create a magic evening space, an outdoor theatre without compare.

In the early 1970s, a major addition was made to the Registry at 24 Princes Street. Designed by John Currie, the original house was built for Alfred Nathan in the 1880s as his family home, 'Wickford'. It was extensively remodelled and extended during the owner's life-time, and following his death in 1931 it became

*Sketch of Registry east wall
in the 1960s before major
additions.*

78

a private hospital, 'Mount Pleasant'. The University obtained it in 1958 to house the Registry, and further additions were made to it in 1967 and 1971. The latter additions comprised four floors at the rear of the building to provide additional office space and a new council room. I sketched the rear of the building in the late 1960s, and at that time was attracted by the gutsy timber verandahs and balustrades related to the masonry wall. The present effete balcony is a sorry reflection of those elements.

The great university building boom of the 1960s had tailed off by the mid 1970s. In some ways this reflected the economy, yet certain committed building projects on or related to the University campus continued in staged construction. The largest of course was the School of Medicine, that great pile of glass-connected buildings that advances towards Grafton Gully like some ghostly grey train. It developed in stages, from 1967 to 1978, though it was officially opened by Her Majesty the Queen in March 1970. The designers, Stephenson & Turner, were the architects also responsible for the earlier Auckland Hospital Clinical Block immediately over Park Road, and for the recently completed nearby Children's Hospital which is appropriately named Starship.

The main pavilion at University Park, Tamaki.

31 Princes Street, once the home of Arthur Nathan, now the base of the Auckland branches of the New Zealand Historic Places Trust and the New Zealand Institute of Architects.

80

7.   The Present

FOR NEARLY a century the Music School was the Cinderella of the University. It had partial use of the Choral Hall and the Grammar School (from 1888 to 1926), and then music lectures and recitals were held in the College Hall of the Princes Street Arts Building. In 1950, the School of Music moved into the Tin Shed vacated by the School of Engineering when it fled the campus and decamped to Ardmore. The Tin Shed was a single-floored, corrugated-iron clad, timber structure hard against the back (west) wall of the Choral Hall.

Nearly twenty years later, the School moved to 31 Princes Street, a plastered brick building ornately decorated. It was built for one John Smith in 1878. In 1896, it became the home of Arthur Hyam Nathan, a wealthy merchant. The lease was purchased from Arthur Nathan's estate in 1917 for £6000 by R. E. N. Russell of the legal firm of Russell McVeagh. 'Pembridge', as 31 Princes Street was named, remained the home of Edward Russell and his family until his death in 1939. Some time later the University acquired the lease, and Pembridge was used both by the Law School and as the senior common room, until the Music School took over in 1969.

I have dwelt on the history of Pembridge, 31 Princes Street, for it is the grandest of the five residences on this prominent road, and is immediately opposite the clock tower of the Arts Building. All these properties belong to the Auckland City Council, and were on a ninety-nine year lease which expired in the 1970s.

In the 1960s, the Auckland City Council sought through an Auckland Improvement Trust Bill to extend Albert Park by removing all but one of the row of nineteenth century houses on the western side of Princes Street. Fortunately, the Bill did not proceed, and this allowed the Music School to move in to Pembridge. It also allowed the preservation of 27 Princes Street, a large residence, substantially altered by Roy Lippincott in 1934, which is now used by Languages International as a School of English. Its northern neighbour is leased by the University Club and was pleasantly converted for that purpose by the design of the architect Denys Oldham.

The School of Music,
Symonds Street.

Though the Music School was far more comfortable in Pembridge, it still lacked sufficient accommodation and had to use 32 Wynyard Street and 18 Grafton Road as teaching and practice studios. Not surprisingly, the desire for a purpose built, permanent home never dimmed. It was ten years before the University Grants Committee allowed a design for a new School of Music to proceed, on the finally determined site in Symonds Street between the Human Sciences Block and St Andrews Presbyterian Church.

The commission was won by Jack Manning and David Mitchell. In *The Elegant Shed*, Mitchell explains how he and Manning, even before they had been sent the brief for the building, discussed a curved masking wall, cut between the

82

relics of the two old buildings on the site, concealing a courtyard. And so it turned out, with the noise-controlling, curved, concrete wall leading to a general, baroque-plan form: a balcony-surrounded courtyard, gently tiered for an outdoor audience (which in fact, it has seldom had). The School is a unique addition to the streetscape, and is regarded highly by students and staff.

The two major additions to the campus designed by JASMAX in the 1980s are the Commerce C Building and the Department of Maori Studies. The former is on the north corner of Symonds Street and Grafton Road, and is a sophisticated complex of related buildings, scaled to simulate the large Victorian residences it replaced, and the two it encompasses so sympathetically: numbers 8 and 10 Grafton Road, the Germanic Languages and Literature Department.

The Music School courtyard.

The Commerce Building, on the corner of Symonds Street and Grafton Road, by JASMaD.

The Commerce C Buildings rise with stepped roof planes away from the corner, the external walls are of cream brick, the roofs orange clay tiles, the windows recessed with extensive use of opaque-coloured glass panels and delightful stained-glass patterned windows to the vertically glazed stairways. The detailing is superb, and one feels that the buildings were lovingly created. This is reflected in the admiration in which they are held within the University and without.

The other building complex by JASMAX, the Department of Maori Studies on the corner of Alten Road and Wynyard Street, is very different. A much smaller venture, it is nevertheless a sensitive grouping of relatively low timber buildings in an L-shape to the south and east of the site. These buildings provide the background to the marae and meeting house which occupy the north-west of the site.

Department of Maori Studies.

O'Rorke Hall, housing 360 student residents, designed by Stephenson and Turner.

The lecture rooms, staff rooms and administration area are accommodated in the L-shaped buildings which are sheathed in vertical cedar boards and battens, and screened where necessary from the westerly sun by verandahs, and at one point by a luxuriant powhiwhi creeper. The meeting house, with its inclined side walls, and the beautiful carving by Dr Paakariki Harrison, must be one of the most outstanding whare runanga in New Zealand. The drama of the marae and meeting house, in colour, form and detail, is enhanced by the muted buildings and plantings which form their background.

O'Rorke Hall, the major university hall of residence, is a recent building of the 1980s, designed by Stephenson & Turner in a burst of post-modernism. It is sited on the corner of Wakefield and Mount Streets, off Symonds Street, occupying part of the land which the University leased in 1948 for £45,000, and replacing the first O'Rorke Hall which had been converted from the former Stonehurst Hotel. This hall of residence grew by gradual expansion from a hundred places to two hundred in the 1970s. The demand for accommodation was twice that available because of its close proximity to the campus and the quite reasonable tariff.

The University in the mid 1980s very wisely purchased the freehold interest of O'Rorke Hall and adjoining land from the Auckland City Council, re-subdivided the entire holding, sold half, and with the proceeds made in those heady days of the property boom, prior to October 1987, was able to build the new O'Rorke Hall and open it debt-free. It has 360 places.

The architects' gallant attempt to provide an interesting form and roof profile, through shape and colour, to this tall residence has succeeded very well. The hall is named for the University College's first chairman, Sir Maurice O'Rorke.

The constraints of the campus, even in its expanded form, have caused some departments such as the Department of Education to become established in buildings outside the recognised campus. This department is now located in leased floors of the Fisher International Building in Waterloo Quadrant, opposite the Old Government House grounds, and immediately to the east of Newman Hall, the University Catholic Chaplaincy building. The first example of the Auckland University occupying a city office building for a major department, it will most certainly not be the last.

In fact, in 1991 the University acquired the lease of two buildings in Eden Crescent, and the freehold of an adjoining third building which had previously been occupied by the Crown as temporary High Court premises. The courts were transferred in 1990-1991 back into the retro-fitted and greatly extended High Court Buildings in Waterloo Quadrant.

These Eden Crescent buildings were, in accordance with a thoroughly detailed brief, converted into the University's Law School, to the design of architects Warren & Mahoney. It is good to see them engaged again on the Auckland campus, or in an area related to it.

The buildings on either side of the centre portion have been converted to staff accommodation and lecture theatres, and are linked by a suspended walkway through the upper level of the centre building, the Law Library. While the Eden Crescent frontages to these three linked buildings have been greatly enhanced, particularly the centre building, through the creation of very deep reveals to the newly recessed windows, the principal frontage from the students' viewpoint is that to the south (facing towards the main campus) at first floor level. The architects

have given this much prominence, with sheltered and planted courts, and no doubt in due course will landscape the rising ground beyond that so the students can climb towards Waterloo Quadrant with reasonable ease. While the Law School is now operating in the new premises, the Library and landscaping were still far from complete in March 1992 when I was sketching there.

The centre building was in earlier days a soda-pop factory, and its conversion to a Law Library is quite masterly. While the ground floor stack-room is ominously low-ceilinged, the new arched, roofed upper floor is more than adequately high to allow for mezzanines, and the earlier mentioned linking walkway.

Here is another example of the University bursting out of its Princes Street

The whare runanga of the Department of Maori Studies, with the Human Sciences Building beyond.

The Law School southern courtyard at first floor level.

89

campus. It is perhaps fitting that the Law School is now very close to the building the University College first occupied in 1883, old Parliament Building.

Already, of course, the University has established a mini campus in south Auckland on the Tamaki site. The student roll at the Princes Street campus now exceeds twenty thousand and the Centre for Continuing Education, located in the Arts Building, has an additional roll of fourteen thousand. It seems inevitable that the student roll will double by the year 2020, and just as inevitable that the Princes Street campus will need to expand, notwithstanding the fact that the Tamaki campus by that time will probably accommodate ten thousand students.

There is clearly space for expansion to the south up Symonds Street and Mount Street. Perhaps Wakefield Street will become the southern boundary of the campus, and there is room for expansion to the north, where Beach Road would become a natural boundary.

The University may also acquire the lease or freehold of sites or buildings in the adjacent central business districts. It has done that in Eden Crescent for the Law School and may just as successfully do the same with sites in High Street, Kitchener Street, Chancery Street or Shortland Street.

One could even contemplate the University absorbing those corner-stones of the campus, St Andrew's and St Paul's, as it becomes increasingly difficult to maintain inner-city congregations no matter how strong the churches may be in members. The successful precedent for this is the 1971 conversion of All Saints Church in Oxford to the Library of the adjoining Lincoln College.

The University of Auckland campus is probably the most successful campus in New Zealand, and that it should be so can be credited to a long line of advocates, academics and politicians, all of whom I hope I have identified in this text.

O'Rorke foremost, with all his glorious failings, was a great advocate of education, and his blind commitment to the promotion of Auckland University at least managed to get it off to a start. The giants thereafter were Leys, and Fowlds, as presidents, and Roy McElroy, the lawyer and one-term Mayor of Auckland, a talented supporter of the Princes Street campus. Of the many parliamentarians involved in the Auckland University campus history, the two whom I regard as most beneficial make strange bedfellows — Sir Joseph Ward and the Hon. Phil Skoglund. Each of these in their different times added direction and firmness to the University's development.

Obviously this same comment is appropriate to the work of Kenneth Maidment and Sir Colin Maiden, the University's two Vice-Chancellors. Equally welcome has been the advocacy of many academics to the logical development and enhancement of the campus. Among these were Sir Algernon Thomas, a foundation professor, Professors H. W. Seagar, Ronald Algie, A. G. Davis, R. T. Kennedy, Richard Toy and Allan Wild.

The Wynyard Café,
Symonds Street.

91

The future of the University of Auckland on the Princes Street site is now assured. The last thirty years have seen reasonably controlled growth. But more important, it now has the goodwill of the community in which it is placed.

The Tamaki campus from University Park, with Mt Wellington beyond.

92

Bibliography

Casson, Hugh, *Hugh Casson's Oxford—A College Notebook*, Phaidon, Oxford, 1988.

Easdale, Nola, *Five Gentlemen's Residences. Princes Street Auckland*, Auckland City Council, 1980.

Fowler, Michael, *The Architecture and Planning of Moscow*, Novosti Press, Moscow, 1980.

Fowler, Michael, *The New Zealand House*, Lansdowne/Rigby, Auckland, 1983.

Fowler, Michael, *Buildings of New Zealanders*, Lansdowne/Rigby, Auckland, 1984.

Hodgson, Terence, *Looking at the Architecture of New Zealand*, Grantham House, Wellington 1990.

Mitchell, David and Chaplin, Gillian, *The Elegant Shed*, Oxford University Press, Auckland, 1984.

Mulgan, Alan, *The Making of a New Zealander*, A. H. & A. W. Reed, Wellington, 1958.

Nalden, Charles, *A History of the Conservatorium of Music. University of Auckland 1881-1981*. (Unpublished).

Nathan, Lawrence D., *As Old as Auckland: The history of L. D. Nathan & Co. Ltd. and of the David Nathan Family 1840-1980*. Benton Ross, Auckland, 1984.

Porter, Frances, (Ed.) *Historic Buildings of New Zealand: North Island*, New Zealand Historic Places Trust, Methuen, Auckland, 1981.

Sinclair, Keith and Mandle, W. F., *Open Account. A History of the Bank of New South Wales in New Zealand 1861-1961*. Whitcomb & Tombs, Wellington, 1961.

Sinclair, Keith, *A History of the University of Auckland 1883-1983*, Auckland University Press, Auckland, 1983.

Stacpoole, John and Beaven, Peter, *Architecture 1820-1970*, A. H. & A. W. Reed, Wellington; 1972.

Stacpoole, John, *William Mason*. Auckland University Press, Auckland, 1971.

Stone, R. C. J., *The Making of Russell McVeagh, 1863-1988*, Auckland University Press, Auckland, 1991.

Tritenbach, Paul, *Botanic Gardens and Parks in New Zealand—An Illustrated Record*, Excellence Press, 1987.

Webb, Beatrice, *Visit to New Zealand in 1898. Beatrice Webb's diary with entries by Sydney Webb*, Price Milburn, Wellington, 1959.

Index